5 DOVER DIGITAL DESIGN S

GRANDVILLE'S ANIMALS

DOVER PUBLICATIONS, INC.
MINEOLA, NEW YORK

The CD-ROM in this book contains all of the images. Each image has been saved as a high-resolution JPEG and an Internet-ready JPEG. There is no installation necessary. Just insert the CD into your computer and call the images into your favorite software (refer to the documentation with your software for further instructions).

Within the "Images" folder on the CD you will find two additional folders—"High Resolution JPG" and "JPG." Every image has a unique file name in the following format: xxx.JPG. The first 3 characters of the file name correspond to the number printed with the image in the book. The last 3 letters of the file name, JPG, refer to the file format. So, 001.JPG would be the first file in the folder.

Also included on the CD-ROM is Dover Design Manager, a simple graphics editing program for Windows that will allow you to view, print, crop, and rotate the images.

For technical support, contact:
Telephone: 1 (617) 249-0245
Fax: 1 (617) 249-0245
Email: dover@artimaging.com
Internet: **http://www.dovertechsupport.com**
The fastest way to receive technical support is via email or the Internet.

Bibliographical Note

Dover Digital Design Source #5: Grandville's Animals, first published by Dover Publications, Inc., in 2010, contains a selection of images from *Scènes de la vie privée et publique des animaux* (1842) and *Les Animaux* (1868), both published by J. Hetzel et Paulin, Paris, and *Un Autre Monde* (1844), published by H. Fournier, Paris. The original French captions were translated to English by Stanley Appelbaum for the Dover edition.

Dover Electronic Clip Art®

International Standard Book Number
ISBN-13: 978-0-486-99069-9
ISBN-10: 0-486-99069-9

Manufactured in the United States by Courier Corporation
99069901
www.doverpublications.com

NOTE

Jean-Ignace-Isidore Grandville (1803–1847) was one of the most fantastic and intriguing artists of early nineteenth-century France. His satirical and humorous caricatures of animals and humans continue to be an inspiration to cartoonists and illustrators. This collection contains a selection of 308 illustrations from some of Grandville's most popular publications, including his most famous work, *Les Animaux*. These whimsical animals with human emotions touch on subject matter such as politics, social customs, the growth of capitalism, Romantic opera and ballet, and social inequalities. The original French captions, translated to English by Stanley Appelbaum, accompany these unusual images.

GRANDVILLE'S ANIMALS

001
Field artillery manned by a dog, a mole, and two crayfish.

002
Part title illustration.

003
The monkey, as editor-in-chief, receives autobiographical manuscripts from the animals; the book will consist of these stories.

004
The monkey-locksmith frees the zoo animals so they can attend a general deliberative assembly.

005

The parrot, who kept the minutes of the animals' assembly, proclaims his secrets from the housetops.

006

Addressing the assembly, the lion urges the animals to shun mankind by living in the wilderness of Africa.

007

At the assembly the chameleon assures the animals that he agrees with each one of them.

4

008
A civet cat offers a pinch of snuff to an elderly beaver.

009
The assembled animals discuss the suggestion that they publish their life stories.

010
A committee (fox, pelican, boar, and eagle) asks
Grandville to illustrate the animals' stories.

011
The birds discuss their editorial responsibilities.

012
A fly writes the "History of Animal Revolutions."

013
The busy advertising and subscription office of the animals' publishing house.

014
The first installment of the animals' book is
sold by street hawkers.

015
Animal sign-painters and bill-posters advertising
the publication of their volume.

016
The magpie, who wrote the hare's story from his dictation.

017
The hare dictating his life story to the magpie.

018
A female bird, in a liberty cap, standing up
for women's rights.

019
Shown with his grandchildren, the old hare, already bitten by a dog, hastens to tell his tale before hunting season.

020
An evil owl blocking the way of two young hares and their sister.

021
The royal lackey who becomes the hare's first owner.

022
A patrol of the National Guard looking askance at revelers
leaving a low-class drinking establishment.

023
After the 1830 revolution, the hare supports his ruined master by playing the drum and doing other tricks.

024
Aristocratic life continues in the Tuileries gardens.

025
The hare's new master, the timorous government clerk.

026
Mister Vulture, the hard-hearted landlord of the government clerk.

027
The pugnacious rooster who insists on fighting a duel with the hare.

028
The rooster awakening the bulldog.

029
Two mice take the English female cat Beauty to a
gathering of literary bluestockings.

030
Beauty's respectable mistress.

031
A young friend of the family asked to sing
at an evening entertainment.

032
Beauty meets Puff, her aristocratic future husband.

13

034
Beauty with her gallant French lover, Brisquet.

033
When Beauty becomes lovesick, the first doctor
called in proposes curing her with an enema.

035
Beauty on trial for adultery.

036
A raven coroner declares that Brisquet, who was really assassinated, poisoned himself.

037
The hymenopteran governess of the young butterfly whose life she relates.

038
Attempting to touch the rose, the butterfly is pricked by her thorns.

039
The butterfly abandons the daisy, who refuses to leave her beloved home.

040
A damsel-fly inspires love in the butterfly's heart.

041
The marriage of the butterfly and the damsel-fly.

042
Guests "hastening" to the wedding party of the butterfly and the damsel-fly.

043
Acrobats entertain the guests at the wedding party.

044
A concert at the wedding party.

045
An old butterfly.

046
The faithless damsel-fly is captured by an insect collector.

047
The food-and-drink loving crocodile who is brought to
Paris after Napoleon's conquest of Egypt.

048
Convivial crocodiles at a banquet.

049
The crocodile's gluttonous owner.

050
The crocodile's owner plans to convert him into a
crocodile pâté, but he escapes.

051
The death's-head moth gives the signal for the silkworm's
funeral procession to begin.

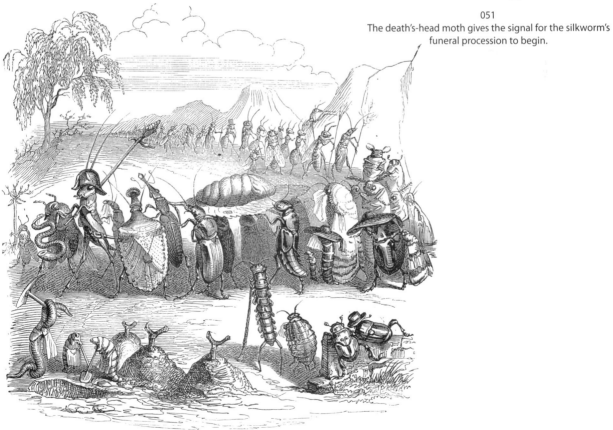

052
The silkworm's funeral procession.

053
A silk mill.

054
The burial of the silkworm.

055
The fearless proletarian Parisian sparrow, who will travel in search of the best type of government, meditates while resting on a statue.

056
The sparrow leaves on his fact-finding mission.

057
The officious customs inspectors on the presumably
libertarian island of the ants.

058
The island of the ants [satire on England].

059
A military officer of the
empire-building ants.

060
In the sinister divine monarchy of the bees.

061
A sentinel in the wolves' republic on the steppes of Russia
(a stronghold of rapacious but free revolutionaries).

062
Fraternity among the wolves.

063
The sparrow now admires the she-wolf who was "the mother of Rome."

064
Equality among animals in the wolves' republic.

065
The hatching of the philosophical auk.

066
The auk arrives on terra firma.

067
The lonely auk is joined briefly by playful birds.

068
The lovesick auk tries to drown himself, but he swims too well.

069
Penguin Island, where (a booby tells him) the auk will feel more at home.

28

070
Blown off course by a storm, the auk reaches Happy Island,
site of a socialist commune, some members of which are
"friends of vegetables."

071
On Happy Island, all children are reared communally
—by serpents and other dangerous animals.

072
A study hall on Happy Island.

073
A former blacksmith now sells comfortable leather
or cloth shoes to horses.

074
The king of Penguin Island.

075
The royal princess, a female auk, whom the king wishes to
marry to the visiting auk.

076
The king of Penguin Island among his subjects.

077
Back from a trip, the auk finds he has two more children than when he left.

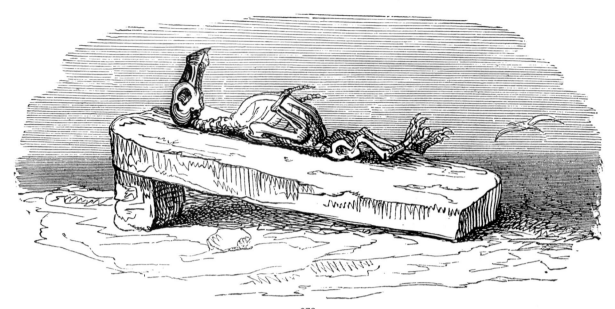

078
Like everyone else, the auk never found real happiness.

079
The praying mantis believes that to die is to be reborn into a better life.

080
The toad who recounts his sad story of loneliness
and rejection.

081
A respectable elderly toad.

082
A duck family comes to the young toad's swimming hole.

083
The kingfisher scolds the toad for frightening away the fish.

084
The porcupine, a disagreeable neighbor of the toad.

085
The beautiful grasshopper whom the toad
saves from a child's net.

086
A handsome fellow who despises the toad's ugliness.

087
The toad and the kingfisher are both fond of bees.

088
Dogs outdoors on a hot day, among them Pistolet,
whose owner is a drama critic.

089
A great Romantic playwright, who gets
all his ideas from others.

090
In old Spanish costume, a noble courtier in the animals' play.

091
The climax of the play: the noble heroine still loves the hero even when he is disheveled and grimy.

092
Birds and snakes in the audience hissing and whistling at the villain.

093
In the fifth act, the jealous husband has become a tiger.

094
The critic Pistolet in the foyer of the theater after the play.

095
Pistolet in his box in the theater.

096
Dogs mourn Pistolet, who has
died of boredom.

097
The old philosophical rat prepares a meal for
his guest, a former ward of his.

098
The old rat's housekeeper, who loves
to mend socks.

099
The misfortunes of rats: indigent, they are refused aid by the greedy rich.

100
The resourcefulness of rats: with courage and brains
they can escape from traps and cats.

101
A poor "church rat" who hands out holy water
and sells tapers.

102
The wise rat thumbs his nose at the world's alarms.

103
A click-beetle on a pin that has the form
of a peony leaf.

104
The wise old owl to whom the beetle tells his story.

105
The capricorn beetle, or sorcerer, predicts that the click-beetle will always see through social problems.

106
The man-about-town June bug who introduces the click-beetle into high society.

107
A grand concert, with a virtuoso pianist.

108
A painting of the animalcules that live in a drop of water.

109
Insects serving some compulsory time in the National Guard.

110
Insects in the National Guard.

111
The fox hero of the learned orangutan's story.

112
The orangutan is told the fox's story by the peculiar ape who had been arranging his bookcases.

113
The ape praises the pleasures of line fishing, where meditation is more important than catching anything.

114
Fisher folk.

115
The ape also praises the pleasures of
butterfly hunting.

116
The young fox hauled before the dog landowner
for stealing grapes.

117
The kind landowner (wearing a mayor's sash) forgives
the fox and teaches him morality.

118
The foxes on a raid eat soft-boiled eggs while the
mother hen weeps.

119
The fox fruitlessly seeks the hen's affections.

120
The fox was really a villain who wanted to eat the hen himself.

121
A young bird wearing a dunce cap.

122
The fox lamenting the hen, who was slaughtered by a human being for food.

123

In the country, the donkey emulates his schoolteacher owner, and teaches classes himself.

124

In Paris, the schoolmaster is advised to become a lecturer on natural history, passing his donkey off as a zebra of an unknown species.

125

An academician comes to examine the rare animal.

126
The schoolteacher will become more than a mere school
monitor taking his pupils for walks in the country.

127
The famous old naturalist refuses to accept the
schoolteacher's revolutionary new theory.

128
A disciple of the schoolteacher gives popular
lectures on the new theory.

129
The ex-schoolteacher, now an illustrious man of
learning and a political power.

130

Some day the fake zebra will gain immortality as a stuffed exhibit in a museum of natural history.

131
The theater clarinetist who will become the narrator greyhound's husband.

132
A female greyhound who tells her story.

133
The highly fashionable public park in which the greyhound strolls.

134
The handsome insect who flirts with the greyhound (tired of her husband, she claims to be a widow).

135
The greyhound and her wooer see exhibitors of performing June bugs.

136
The greyhound and her wooer see a bear
leading a performing tortoise; the bear is her
husband in disguise.

137
The greyhound's husband, who assailed her
wooer, has been arrested.

138
A miscellaneous animal fantasy.

139
A miscellaneous animal grouping.

140
In Paris, the Brazilian monkey Topaz
becomes an artist's assistant.

141
Topaz on his way to an art lesson.

142
Devoid of inspiration, Topaz becomes a daguerreotypist; his first important
satisfied sitter is a bear, who gives his portrait to his sweetheart.

143
Topaz retouches a daguerreotype in his studio, to
a chorus of comments by gawkers.

145
Topaz taking a picture

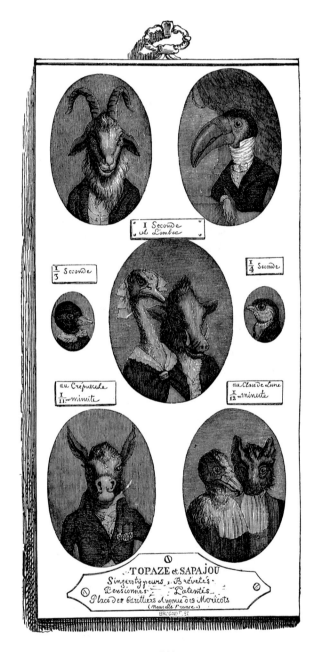

144
Pictures of Topaz's customers.

146
Sick of his customers' unjustified complaints, Topaz drowns himself.

147
An African lion journeys to Paris on a diplomatic mission; he is
sent by his father, the king, to get him out of the way.

148
The old king and his court.

149
The dog who shows the lion around Paris.

150
A café scene.

151
A lion (dandy) of Paris with his young page.

152
A lionne of Paris.

153
A scene at a Carnival ball.

154
In Carnival season, "animal passions break
out in man."

155
"People care more about entertainers than about liberty."

156
The closing of the original first volume: the reader is bidden to go home and sleep tight.

157
First part-title of the original second volume.

158
Second part-title of the original second volume.

159
Amid a revolt against the former animal editors, the fox becomes sole editor.

160
Animals faithful to the old editors on the lookout for trouble.

161
A beetle reading the paper issued by the old editors
during the troubles.

162
In the first stage of the revolt, loyal bumblebees ward
off hostile flies and wasps.

163
The hostile insects' buglers.

164
The seditious gnats having indulged in oratory about sacrificing
their heads, the vulture examines the value of such heads.

165
The Hercules beetle, leader of the rebellious insect forces.

166
During the troubles, assemblies of gregarious animals such as ducks are dispersed by the authorities.

167
Law-abiding people who stay home and mind their own business.

168
An elephant, whom one would have considered "above such things," joins the conspiracy.

169
The bison speaks out at a meeting of the rebels.

170
Another fiery orator demanding speedy action.

During the revolt, walls are covered with political manifestos.

The fox receives the rebels' oath that they
will settle matters on the following day.

Three penguins lead a numerous troop of marching rebels.

174
A citizen militia is called out to preserve order.

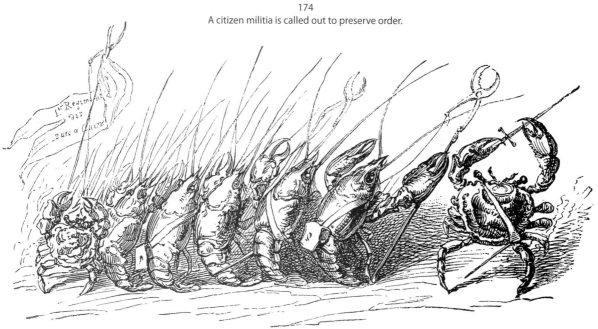

175
A crab leads crayfish auxiliaries in defense of the status quo.

176
The toad appeals to patriotic feelings.

177
A loyal guardian of the old regime on sentry duty.

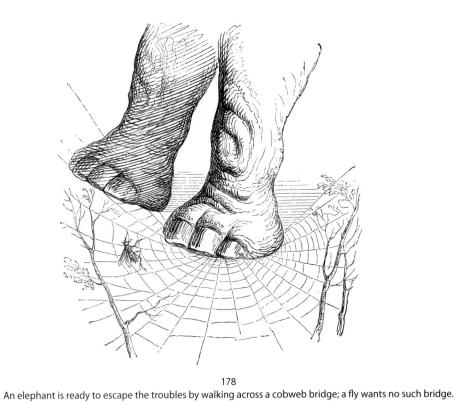

178
An elephant is ready to escape the troubles by walking across a cobweb bridge; a fly wants no such bridge.

179
The heavy infantry of the rebellious insects.

180
A rebel wasp stabs a loyalist June bug, and the
loyalist insect army flees.

181
The good weather is on the side of the rebels—
why won't it rain?

182
The fox takes over the editorship and
addresses his well-wishes.

183
The rebels storm the animals' editorial office.

184
A committee of zoo notables visits the fox.

185
At the rebels' victory banquet, the showy
hoopoe acts as steward.

186
A gallant gentleman toasts the fair sex.

187
After the fox is in power, the animals continue to draw up
many petitions, which are systematically ignored.

188
The white blackbird [proverbial for a great rarity]
who will tell his life story.

189
As his mother weeps, the young white blackbird is
disowned by his father.

190
The compassionate magpie who aids
the white blackbird.

191
The magpie and the dove come to the aid of the
exhausted white blackbird.

192
The cockatoo poet, who is too egoistic to care about the white blackbird.

193
Nighttime in a forest outside Paris.

194
An unfriendly old dove, one of the birds encountered
in the woods by the white blackbird.

195
Wanton thrushes prove to be unsuitable company for the blackbird.

196
In Paris, the blackbird overhears two concierges praising the value of a "white blackbird," and he gains self-respect.

198
The blackbird discovers his wife's cosmetic secrets.

197
The white blackbird, now a famous author, marries an English blackbird who claims to be white like him.

199
The bee who narrates his life story.

200
Beetles resting.

201
A bee nursemaid in the hive giving her charges bread and honey.

202
The bee, in love with a drone, wishes she was
as attractive as a dragonfly.

203
She'd also like to be one of those elegantly narrow-waisted
wasps one meets in society.

204
Professor Granarius declares that rationality causes all the ills of society.

205
The professor with a paper container of scale insects which
he will place on a cactus (they will colonize it as parasites).

206
The professor's daughter Anna,
hopelessly in love with his young assistant.

207
The male cochineal insect rejecting the advances of imperfect mates.

208
A volvox epidemic strikes the near-microscopic world of the scale insects.

209
A renewed volvox attack.

210
Guards encircle the ideal mate, who is still in the larval stage.

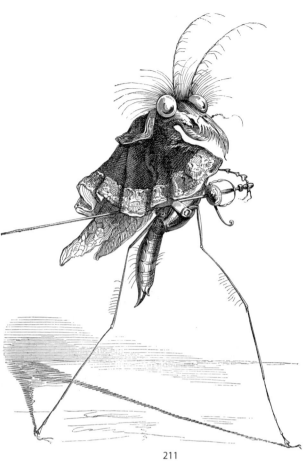

211
A strange insect called the "misocamp," fond of eating scale insects.

212
The courtship of the scale insects.

213
The ugly and silly heiress whom the professor's
upwardly mobile assistant marries.

214
The professor is pleased with his success in producing cochineal, while Anna laments her sweetheart's betrayal.

215
The cat Minette writes letters to her sister Bébé.

216
Bébé's poor mistress, who lives by sewing.

217
The messenger who delivers a letter from Minette to Bébé.

218
When the sisters were younger, their mistress once gave them a toy mouse.

219
Minette pays more attention to her evil genius, who promises wealth, than to her guardian angel.

220
Married to Brisquet, Minette lives in the lap of luxury.

221
Minette is now rich enough to own a fur muff!

222
The exotic Chinese cat for whom Brisquet deserts Minette.

223
Though widowed, Minette turns a deaf ear to Toms who come courting.

224
A family scene among the animals.

225
Phrenological specimens with unexpected character traits.

226
A stork presiding over a session of assizes.

227
Testimony in a case involving a poisoned toad: the
mole accuses the viper.

228
In jail, accused of killing a ewe and a lamb, the wolf reads pastoral poetry.

229
When the wolf is convicted, broadsheets appear recounting his crime in moralistic platitudes.

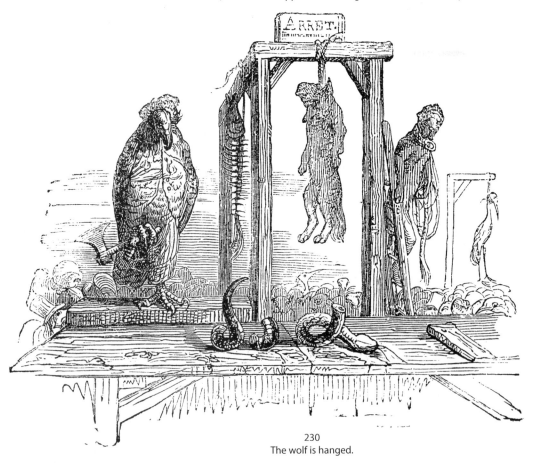

230
The wolf is hanged.

231
The lame young bear is withdrawn and melancholy.

232
The bear living alone in the mountains.

233
When the bear is acquired by an innkeeper, he
dances with village maidens.

234
After many more adventures, the bear enjoys life
in the bosom of his family.

235
The "seventh heaven," beyond the clouds.

236
The passing of the turtledove, according to his own
posthumous narration; the bird of prey represents Death.

237
The turtledove had been orphaned
while still very young.

238
His fickle sweetheart had become the
mother of a numerous brood.

239
The turtledove had turned into a solitary dreamer.

240
Swallows migrating from Paris.

241
A bird of passage who will deliver the swallow's
letters to her domestically contented canary
friend in Paris.

242
The swallow meets a nightingale tenor who advises her
to live for pleasure.

243
An elderly bird with a reputation for great wisdom.

244
The problems faced by an authoress mother.

245
Tragedy in a robin family: a fledgling falls from the nest while a bird of prey is near.

246
A poacher bags the bird of prey.

247
A shrike, stepmother of two warblers, makes their life miserable.

248
A shy young woodcock sings a song of her own composition at a literary gathering.

249
The swallows return to Paris in the spring.

250
The crippled old dog telling his story to the editor fox.

251
The sick dog, attended by a sow, has his case discussed by the diagnosticians: a sloth, a leech, a dugong, a crane, a Spanish fly and others.

252
In the hospital, the surgeons are a shark and a sawfish, and the medical students are rats, ravens and vultures.

253
A medical student.

254
A disabled ex-soldier in front of the Hôtel des Invalides.

255
The old dog's future grave.

256
An animal fantasy.

257
The giraffe in the Paris zoo, a gift from the ruler of
Egypt, with one of the cows who nursed her.

258
Military men use artificial weapons, lacking natural ones.

259
Scholars bury themselves in books that become their chrysalis.

260

In her letter, the giraffe mistakes the monkey house in the zoo for the Chamber of Deputies in session.

261
Two modern lovers in the zoo.

262
Animals bringing complaints.

263
No human being would accept a
mother kangaroo's burdens.

264
No human beings have such a close family life
as hibernating marmots do.

265
Opera ballerinas are renowned for
their shrewdness.

266
Defenseless hares shouldn't be
called cowardly.

267
Songbirds (like the nightingale who loves the rose) have as much soul as human beings.

268
Only in human society are there beggars and street musicians.

269
The raven who has been making all these complaints about human beings.

270
Animals traveling for various reasons.

271
The husband of the memoir-writing crow dies at the Strasbourg cathedral; the stork advises her to travel.

272
The crow sets down her travel experiences.

273
The banker who purchases an old château and has parts of it repaired.

274
An up-to-date hunter.

275
The bats and the fashionable owls who live in
the restored part of the château.

276
The falcon who lives in the unrepaired part
of the château.

277
A neighbor and protégé of the falcon—a field mouse
occupied with burrowing.

278
Petty modern hunters (in contrast with the falcon's memories
of grand hunts).

279
The falcon's only servant, a starling.

280
During her stay at the château, the crow studies
the ways of a lizard.

281
The idle, dreamy lizards who live in the old wing
of the château.

282
The lizard's wife suspects that there's more to life, though she doesn't know what it can be.

283
The ridiculous female owl who lived in the altered wing of the château.

284
After his wife has run off, the male owl consults a fortune-telling carp for advice and witnesses this scene of divination.

285
The crow family finds happiness with an old childhood friend.

286
The fox, the new editor of the animals' stories, is overwhelmed by complaints.

287
A new animal rebellion is quashed by human
authorities, and the animals return to the zoo.

288
The turtledoves still have love to console
them, and they fly to the clouds.

289
Back in his lair, the bear abandons politics and becomes a nursemaid to his children.

291
The animals make a bonfire of their remaining manuscripts.

290
The dog goes back to playing the part of a blind man with
a small organ and a cup for alms.

292
Under the watchful eye of his keeper is the hedgehog-bulldog hybrid called the journalist.

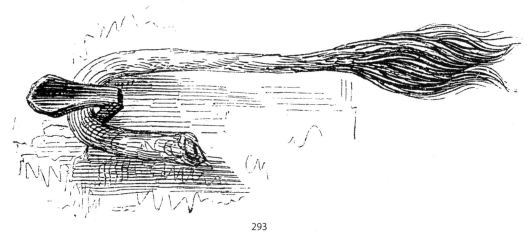

293
Animal tailpiece.

294
The undersea carnival procession of the fatted ox.

295
At the undersea ball, a male lamb dances with an aging female panther, a fox casts loving glances at a hen, and a partridge captivates a hound with her gaze.

296
At the ball, a hare attacks a lioness, a gazelle drags by his mane her lion-lover who has paid too much attention to a ballerina-greyhound, and a raven in a black domino tells jokes.

297
Before the tolerant eyes of the police, an adolescent duck-frog performs a very free dance with an owl-mouse.

298
At a more aristocratic undersea ball visited by Krackq, the animals masquerade as human beings rather than as other animals.

299
A "pas de crabes" in the grand Romantic ballet *The Loves of Venus,* in which the nymphs of the corps de ballet are mice and grasshoppers, while the Cyclopes (who perform a hammer dance) are scarab beetles.

300
Fish fishing for people, using various desirable items as bait.

301
A dog walking his man.

302
The Duchess of Sorrel with two of her English thoroughbreds, one mounted by her mechanically miniaturized groom.

303
An academic teacher of painting and his pupils, mounted on a Raphael hobbyhorse, trace details from the old masters.

304
The centaur, with his turtle-hound, in pursuit of a boa-bear.

305
The cages of heraldic animals.

306
The pit of "doublivores" (animals that can eat at both ends) at the zoo.

307
The bird collection at the zoo.

308
The animals entering the steam ark.